# Query

*Everything you need to get started, get noticed, and get signed.*

*By: C.J. Redwine*

# My Querying Experience

The first time I typed those magical words "The End" on a manuscript, I was a tiny bit surprised when the heavens refused to open up and bathe my glorious novel in brilliant light while somewhere in the distance angels sang the Hallelujah chorus. I mean, I had <u>done it</u>. Started a story and followed it through to its conclusion thousands of words later. That's a huge accomplishment, right?

Right.

The heavens refused to cooperate, but that didn't mean the publishing world wouldn't sit up and take notice, right?

Wrong.

Turns out there were hundreds of other writers who'd proudly typed "The End," and they were all vying for a space on the bookshelf. And editors at all the major houses were closed to any unagented submissions. I couldn't get my work in front of the kind of industry professional I was looking for without help. I needed a literary agent.

A little bit of research on the Internet and one writer's conference later, I realized the only way to snag an agent was to write a query letter. There were many vague descriptions and instructions lurking on various web sites, but none of them broke down the querying process and told me "Do A" and then "Do B" and for the love of all commas, don't you dare "Do C." Without some hard and fast instructions, I began experimenting.

My first query letter was a solid, wordy piece of hopelessly uninteresting horse pucky. I felt the need to introduce every character who graced my pages. Every. Character. And if I was going to introduce them, well then by golly, I should explain their function. And the setting was important too, wasn't it? And what about conflict? Should I put in the major external conflict or the various inner conflicts? Or maybe, when those didn't sound quite as good as I thought they should, toss in a conflict that wasn't currently in the book but <u>could be</u> if the agent asked for a partial? I put every possible detail I could cram onto a page (10 point font, baby!) and sent that sucker out.

Then I waited. I twiddled my thumbs. Pretended to write while really I was perfecting my prowess at Plants vs. Zombies. Obsessively checked blogs and websites of agents I'd queried. And finally, the responses began pouring in. Rejections. Every single one of them.

That was fun. So much fun, I probably shouldn't ever do it again because no one deserves to have that much fun twice in one lifetime.

I decided my query letter was to blame, and tried to revise. But I still didn't know what to leave out and what to include. And the exercise of trying to reduce my 95k novel into a pithy little summary left me feeling like yanking out the hair on my head one at a time would be much more enjoyable.

It was about this time that a website run by a literary agent hosted a query contest. Writers could post their queries and await the sharp teeth of the literary agent. If she happened to love it, she'd request pages. If she didn't, she'd be honest with you on the reasons why. I signed up, half expecting her to love mine.

She didn't. Neither did she hate it. I'd managed to write a query that was as forgettable as a scoop of store-brand vanilla ice cream. She advised me to cut the clichés (turns out my plot was full of them.), focus in on my main characters, and show her why she should care enough to keep reading.

That was excellent advice. By this time, I'd sent out another round of queries and been soundly rejected again, and I was learning how to grow a thick skin. Putting my thick skin to use, I took a good, hard look at my novel and realized that what I'd originally thought was my entree into the world of publishing was, in fact, a learning ground for me to begin honing my craft. I set the book aside and sat down to write another.

When I finished, I turned my attention to learning the skill of writing an excellent query hook. It took me several drafts before I finally tossed out everything I thought I knew about queries, and went with gut instinct instead. My gut told me readers responded to voice and high stakes. So, I revised until I had a query I felt delivered both.

The same literary agent was now running a site called Query Shark (http://queryshark.blogspot.com) where she did nothing but critique drafts of queries readers submitted. I sent in my query, fingers crossed that I'd learned my earlier lessons, and within four hours, she'd emailed me to request a partial. I turned around and queried eight other agents I'd been researching. Seven of them requested pages as well.

Shortly after that, I signed with my agent. I figured I was done with writing hooks, but then as I spent time with writers, read messages on loops, or paid attention on Twitter, I realized that many, many others were struggling with the art of query writing. I remembered how much I wished someone would just TELL ME how to do it, break it down for me in manageable steps, and teach me the lessons I had to learn the hard way. I began offering online courses where I did exactly that for my clients. Before long, my classes were filling up within days of offering a new one, and I was being invited to speak at writer's groups and conferences. I loved helping others unlock the mysteries of querying, and it thrilled me to hear about former clients finding agents and then selling books.

But when I signed a book deal of my own and looked at my upcoming deadlines, I realized I couldn't commit to a monthly workshop schedule any longer. So, I decided to put my lessons and experience into a handbook other writers could use in the quest to find the right path to publication. I encourage you to practice, revise, try new approaches, and above all, never stop believing in yourself as you embark on the difficult, rewarding, and often times surreal experience of Querying.

## What is a Query Letter?

A query letter is a one page introduction of you and your book to prospective agents or editors. The goal is to entice the agent or editor to request pages. The letter follows basic business letter format, but the content needs to be the equivalent of a back-of-the-book hook. You must stay within this one page format, and a smart writer uses plenty of white space to break up the type and increase the pacing, which means you must be careful to include only the essentials. Remember, a query letter is designed to sell your book to your reader, and books sell on concept and hook, not on a deluge of information.

## How Do I Know When I'm Ready To Query?

Have you finished writing a book? If not, you aren't ready to query. You should never query without a completed, polished draft ready to send to an agent or editor who expresses interest.

Have you walked away from your manuscript for at least a month and then returned to revise it until it begins to look like the book you meant to write in the first place? If not, you aren't ready to query. You want your draft to be in the best condition possible before you send it out. No one's first draft is their best. Don't make the mistake of querying too soon! It's better to wait until you're sure of your product. The literary agents and editors you're interested in will still be there once you've finished revising.

Do you have a thick skin? I mean it. Do you? You're going to get rejected. If Nora Roberts, Dean Koontz, and J.K. Rowling all received a slew of rejections, you have to be prepared to do the same. Let's be honest. Rejections suck. Even the nice ones. But if you've chosen to pursue publication, you've chosen a profession that specializes in rejection at every stage. Smart writers learn a) how to take what is helpful from a rejection and use it to hone their craft, b) how to respond professionally, and c) how to keep a pile of rejections from plunging them into a pit of despair, thereby compromising their ability to write.

Do you know what you want out of your writing career? If you don't have at least a five year plan, I suggest making one. Will you want to write a series? Do you want to be published in multiple genres? How many quality books can you legitimately produce a year? Do you prefer to work with someone who is hands on or someone who has a more cut and dried approach? Do you love to communicate through email or do you prefer phone calls? These are just some of the questions you might want to ask yourself before querying. You need to research agents who fit what you want to do with your career, not just the ones that fit the book you're about to send out.

Is your online presence professional? Don't make the mistake of thinking an interested agent or editor won't Google you. They will. They want to know if your Facebook page has pictures of that one time you drank too many margaritas and decided to do karaoke sans clothing. They want to see if you've left a trail of nasty, author-bashing reviews across Amazon. They wonder if you've taken to your blog to slam the other agents or editors who rejected your project. Why are they looking for things like this? Because publishing is a business of relationships, and no one wants to work with someone who might be a high maintenance diva with a poor sense of discretion. Make your less-than-professional photos private. Clean up your blog, Twitter, and other web presences to make sure you're completely professional. You can still be fun and interesting! But you can't be vicious, whiny, or bitter without making an agent or editor think twice before asking for your pages.

So, do you have a finished, polished manuscript, a thick skin, a career plan, and a professional web presence? If so, congratulations and strap on your seat belt. You're ready to query!

## What Would Having An Agent Do For Me?

Do you really need a literary agent? That depends on what you want out of your career. No one can answer that question for you, but I can list the things a good agent would do for you so you can make the best decision for yourself. Typically, a literary agent's contract with a writer stipulates that the agent gets paid 15% of the writer's domestic income, and 20% of foreign and film sales. So, what does an agent do to earn this money?

- A good agent helps you shape your manuscript to get it into the best possible shape before sending it out to editors. Please note this is in addition to the edit you did yourself before you queried.
- A good agent is an expert on the market, and knows the ins and outs of the genres he or she represents.
- A good agent has relationships built with editors at publishers across New York and beyond. The agent knows which editors are looking for specific types of projects, which editors usually respond favorably to a project like yours, and which editor's working style most closely matches how you prefer to write.
- A good agent understands how to maximize the submissions process to generate the most interest and therefore the best deal for your book. Sometimes this means an agent gives a specific editor an exclusive in hopes of getting a pre-empt offer to take the project off the table before others get a look at it. Sometimes this means an agent juggles interest from several parties and uses that interest to push each house to put their best offer on the table.
- A good agent negotiates fiercely to help you get the most out of any offer. There are a lot of miscellaneous things on the table besides an advance and the number of books a house is willing to buy up front. Who keeps foreign rights? Film and tv rights? Audio rights? Will your books have separate accounting or will you have to earn out the entire advance before you see another dime? What happens if you need to convince a publisher to give

you back the rights to out of print books? A good agent knows how to handle all of that.

- A good agent is committed to your career growth, not just to one project. He or she is invested in helping you choose wisely which projects to focus on, which houses to submit to, when and if self-publishing is the right choice for a project, and any other career decisions that crop up.
- A good agent negotiates foreign rights sales and film rights sales. He or she has contacts and co-agents in those industries and works those contacts to produce more sales for you. He or she also negotiates those contracts to get the best deal for you.
- A good agent reads your contracts with an eagle eye and works with the publisher until all terms are something you can agree to.
- A good agent remains a valuable resource throughout the publishing process, especially if issues arise over cover art or deadlines or any of the other nine hundred small details that make up the publishing process for one book.
- A good agent always acts as your advocate, is in your corner, and is constantly monitoring the market, the publishing houses, and your own personal career plan to help you achieve your goals.

There are a number of smaller presses and e-publishers who don't require agented submissions, and you may choose to submit to them directly (In which case, you'll still need an amazing query!). Or, you may decide you need an advocate in the publishing world and that a literary agent is right for you. If so, it's time to learn how to research the agents you'd like to query.

## Researching Literary Agents

Before I list some resources you might use to research agents, I'd like to take a moment to discuss a few things that are red flags as you look into agencies. If you see any of the following, you may want to pass on querying that agent and move on to another.

- **Reading Fees:** No reputable agent charges a reading fee for any reason. Period. Every legitimate, ethical agent gets paid only when they sell a book for you.
- **No record of sales:** An agent should be able to list specific books he or she has recently sold. Be wary of agents who refer to sales, but have no hard data to back that up. Also, be careful of those who only sell to houses that take unagented submissions, as the agent may simply be picking up clients who already submitted their manuscripts and had an offer on the table before looking for an agent.
- **No membership in AAR:** The Association of Author's Representatives has a code of ethics that legitimate agents and agencies adhere to. If an agent chooses not to be a member of AAR, it doesn't necessarily mean he or she isn't ethical.

But it does mean you need to take a good hard look before proceeding.

- **Exclusive Queries:** This is not the industry standard. Most agents expect you to be sending out simultaneous queries. It's certainly in your best interest to do so, especially considering the lengthy response time many agents have. Consider the cost of the time you'll lose waiting for this agent's response before you decide to query.
- **Editing Services For Hire:** If an agent offers to edit your manuscript for a fee, hold on to your cash. A reputable agent will work with you to whip your manuscript into shape after you've signed a contract without asking for a dime. A legitimate agent only gets paid when you do.
- **Copying or Processing Fee:** Again, you should never be asked to pay money up front. The agency takes care of any fees in conjunction with the submissions process up-front and recoups them only from your advance.
- **Promising the Moon:** If an agent promises you a huge book deal in less than a month or any other promise that smacks of hyperbole, step back and take a hard look at that agent's sales record. A savvy agent never promises anything but to work hard to get your manuscript in front of the right editors.
- **Grammatical Errors:** If an agent's website or communication is full of grammatical or mechanical errors, walk away. You're in the market for someone who will be your

representative in the publishing industry. Even if this agent is legitimate, do you really want someone representing you in that fashion?

- **Poor Communication**: Once you've begun the process of discussing representation with an agent, if you notice a consistent failure to reply to emails, return phone calls, or be on time to appointments, think twice. The agent is trying to make a good impression on you. What will the communication be like when the agent no longer needs to convince you to sign a contract?

Now that you know what red flags to look for, here are some valuable resources to use in researching agents who represent your genre, have a solid track record, and have no ethical or legal complaints lodged against them.

- **WRITER'S MARKET:** This book is a comprehensive list of agents, which agency they belong to, and what they represent, along with any additional information about submissions etc. the agent has elected to include. The book also includes similar information for editors, as well as places to sell freelance or non-fiction projects. Each year the book is updated, so be sure to purchase to very latest and greatest and cross-reference with the agent's website. WRITER'S MARKET also offers a deluxe edition and an edition solely for novelists and short story writers.
- **Attend writer conferences:** There are several highly reputable conferences offered at both a local and national level for writers of every description.

Look for a conference that specializes in your genre, offers workshops taught by published authors, agents, and editors, and gives you the opportunity for face time with agents and editors. You'll benefit from meeting industry professionals, get a good feel for those you'd like to work with, and the relationships you'll build with other writers will help you plug in to the industry in ways you could never manage on your own. Some national writer associations you might be interested in looking at are Romance Writers of America (RWA), Science Fiction and Fantasy Writers of America (SFWA), and Society of Children's Book Writers and Illustrators (SCBWI). There are also regional and local conferences, writing chapters, and events along with online writer's conferences such as WriteOnCon. All of these are excellent places to research agents and editors and build industry relationships. Be wary of any conference that guarantees representation or makes the conference experience seem like anything other than an educational and networking opportunity.

- **Predators & Editors:** Visit the Predators & Editors website to research specific agents and see if there are any legal or ethical complaints lodged against either the agent or the agency. http://pred-ed.com/
- **Writer Beware:** Visit the Writer Beware website to research any red flags listed against agents or agencies. http://accrispin.blogspot.com/
- **Absolute Write:** Visit the Absolute Write website, head to the forums, and see if any agents on your

list are garnering ethical or legal complaints.
http://absolutewrite.com

- **Publisher's Marketplace:** To really use this site, you'll need to pay a membership fee. If you purchase a membership, you can see the deals agents are currently making AND put up a web page showcasing you as a writer. Agents and editors do sometimes browse those pages. That's how J.T. Ellison (best-selling author of the Taylor Jackson series) landed her agent. I personally think the ability to see an agent's track record in domestic and foreign sales is worth the price of membership, but that's a decision you'll need to make for yourself. Not all agents and editors report deals to the site, and some only report a portion of their deals. http://www.publishersmarketplace.com/

- **Agent Query:** This is a site devoted to listing agents, what genres they represent, and what they're currently seeking. Please note that it's possible not every legitimate agent is listed on this site. www.agentquery.com

- **Query Tracker:** This site helps you research agents, see an agent's current response time on queries, partials, and fulls, and track your own submissions and response time. Please note that not all legitimate agents are listed on this site. http://www.querytracker.net/

How many agents do you need to research? That's up to you. But remember, it might take many, many "no's" until you finally get the "yes" you're looking for. A good rule of thumb is to decide how many queries you feel comfortable having out at any given time (For me, that was ten, but you may have a different threshold.) and research enough agents to identify a target list of double that amount. That way, every time a rejection comes in, you can turn around and query the next agent on your list. Nothing beats the sting of rejection like taking positive action.

## Writing A Three Part Query Letter

A query letter needs to accomplish three things. It must let an agent or editor know you're a professional and you've done your research. It must showcase any writing credentials or useful biographical information you have. And it must, above all else, hook an agent or editor on your book. I suggest accomplishing this goal by writing a three part query. When I queried, I preferred to lead with my hook and cover my credentials, genre, title, word count, and why I'd queried that agent at the end of the query. Others like to lead with that information, or perhaps open with why they're querying that particular agent, transition into the hook, and then finish up with the credentials. Feel free to play around with the exact order until you find something that suits you. I'm going to teach you what each element needs to be successful.

### Part One: Why This Agent?

This is your opportunity to stand out from the writers who approach querying as if they're firing a shotgun at the side of a barn hoping to get lucky. YOU did your research. You know why you think this agent is a good fit for your career and for this project. And you're going to tell them in one or two simple sentences. Save your word count for what really matters: your hook.

Here are some generic examples:

"I'm a regular reader of your blog and have long admired your work ethic and sense of humor. When you mentioned last week that you wanted an edgy YA project, I felt my novel might be a good fit for you."

"My goal is to publish both genre adult fiction and middle grade fiction, and because you successfully represent both, I feel you might be the right agent to help me build my career."

"I recently heard you speak on a panel at the SCBWI conference in Nashville. I was impressed with your agency's focus on building long-term careers, and would love the opportunity to work with you."

"Because you represent C.J. Redwine and my books are similar in tone to hers, I feel you might be the right agent for me."

"Your client C.J. Redwine recently read my manuscript and suggested I query you as she felt you might love my book as much as she did."

"I'm impressed with your sales record on Publisher's Marketplace, and would love the opportunity to work with you."

"We met at the RWA conference last week when I pitched my novel DEFIANCE to you. I sincerely enjoyed talking with you, and was especially impressed with your grasp of the YA market."

## Part Two: Bio & Writing Credentials

Want to know a secret? You don't need to stress about your bio and your writing credentials. Many debut writers have very few writing credentials to their name. If you do have some writing credentials, that's great. If you don't, please don't worry about trying to fill the paragraph with degrees and assurances that you've been writing for most of your life. None of that matters. What matters is that you wrote an amazing book, one the agent thinks he or she can sell. You're going to convince the agent of that with your hook. So, stop stressing. This is going to be the easiest part of the entire query. Ready? Here you go.

### <u>What to Include in Your Bio Paragraph</u>:

- Always start your bio paragraph with a one sentence summary of your book's stats. This is simply title, genre, and word count. "DEFIANCE is a young adult novel complete at 95k words." That's it. Don't deviate from this example unless you want to include something like "written in the vein of Kristin Cashore and Alison Goodman." The purpose of this sentence is to give the agent or editor the title, an idea of where it can be shelved in a bookstore, and the word count. If you don't know what genre your book is, do the research to figure it out. You may have written an historical sci-fi with romantic suspense elements, but that isn't a genre in the book store. Choose the prevalent genre as the label in your query. If you've written a middle grade or young adult, simply tack on the extra genre description. (Such as "middle grade fantasy" or "contemporary young adult.") And please, PLEASE, do yourself the favor of Googling industry accepted word counts. If you're significantly below or above the industry standard, you'll have a hard time getting requests.

- List any major writing credentials you might have. Do so in no more than a couple of sentences. Major writing credentials include being previously published in novel or short story length. If you've self-published previous work and the sales figures are significant (over 10,000 copies sold), you can include those details. If you've won or finaled in a significant literary contest, include that. (Not your local paper, not a campus-wide writing contest, but something that is either national or international). If you have a degree in creative writing, feel free to include that. Keep in mind that no degree guarantees you actually have the ability to craft a publishable novel, so if you don't have a fancy degree, it doesn't matter. If you aren't sure whether to include something, here's a good rule of thumb: if it shows that someone with industry experience has recognized literary talent in you, put it in. If you don't have any credentials, don't sweat it. Your hook sells the agent or editor on requesting pages.

- Finish up the paragraph with a polite "Thank you for your time. I look forward to hearing from you." That's it. No gushing about how hopeful you are. No listing of all the different things (Synopsis! Chapters! Full Manuscript!) you can send if the agent or editor is interested. All of that is assumed. No explanations for what writing means to you, how hard you worked on this book, how much you want to touch readers with your story etc. Just thank them professionally and sign your name.

## Part Three: Writing the Hook

The most important element of your query letter is your hook. If you take a look at the book jackets of other books in your genre, you'll notice that books sell on voice and concept. Infusing your hook with your manuscript's voice while delivering the concept is crucial. You don't want this portion of your query to read like a dry, stale business letter. This is your chance to showcase your talent, capture your reader, and leave the agent or editor wanting more.

Understanding your "Voice" can be tricky for newer writers. If you can't look at your book and choose two-three adjectives to describe your style, then grab a few books of authors whose work is similar to yours and describe theirs instead. Most likely, a few of the adjectives you apply to their books can also be applied to yours. Why is it necessary to understand your Voice? Because you need to deliver it in your query. If you write sardonic, edgy paranormal, then your query needs to read like a sardonic, edgy paranormal. If you write lyrical, emotionally rich prose, your query should be lyrical, emotionally rich prose. Spend some time gaining an understanding of the Voice in your manuscript and what it is about your prose and your pacing that makes it YOURS, and you'll be able to duplicate it in your query.

Once you understand your Voice, you'll need to thoroughly understand the heart of your book's concept so you can know exactly what you need to deliver in your query. It is absolutely unnecessary to introduce every character, plot twist, or important detail. In fact, that route leads to Query Death. Keep it simple and full of power. Include the Big Guns only. I'm going to give you a simple method to reduce your novel down to your Big Guns.

At its most basic, a novel's concept is this:

<u>A</u> must do <u>B</u> to avoid or accomplish <u>C</u> but <u>D</u> is a huge problem.

Fill in those blanks to narrow your manuscript down into one tidy concept. And by fill in the blanks, I mean with a word, a phrase, or a sentence at the most. Be concise. This sentence is NOT your hook. It's designed to show you what must go into your hook—your main characters, their agenda, and the huge impossible thing that is standing in their way.

Here's an example using Harry Potter and The Deathly Hallows:

<u>Harry</u> must <u>find and destroy the remaining Horcruxes</u> to <u>defeat Voldemort</u> but <u>the fact that he must remain hidden,</u>

the lack of information on the Horcruxes, and Voldemort's increasing power over the world are a huge problem.

Once you have your basic concept identified and you understand the Voice of your manuscript, it's time to start drafting your hook. Sometimes it takes several drafts before you finally get it right. Don't be afraid to experiment a bit until you feel you've pushed yourself to be as specific as possible about the story set-up (no generic clichés!), and you've delivered the high stakes in your novel. Here are some suggestions for writing a stellar hook:

- **Use this simple structure**: One small paragraph introducing your hero/heroine, one small paragraph introducing the love interest (if applicable), one small paragraph showing how things get crazy/difficult/go WRONG, and a small paragraph showing what the hero and heroine must do to overcome their obstacles and what it will cost them if they don't.
- **Always introduce your main character first**. Give us a quick glimpse into that character's personality and life situation so your reader can identify with him/her. A "quick glimpse" is a sentence or two. i.e. "Sarah Hightower—cheerleader, prom queen, and valedictorian of her senior class—has a secret that could kill her." In one sentence, I've introduced the main character, set up that she's a popular girl who gets what she wants, knows how to work hard, and is used to succeeding, and I've snagged the reader's attention with the revelation that the seemingly perfect Sarah is hiding something terrible.

- **Flesh out your main character's situation in just a few sentences**: You need just enough to set up the situation and help the reader feel a sense of connection to your hero or heroine. Keep it simple and powerful. We don't need five sentences of backstory when with a little effort, you can deliver the set-up in a phrase or two. If you feel overwhelmed at the thought of doing this, make a list of everything you think the reader needs to know about this character and the story set-up. Then combine items or eliminate less important ones until you have five things or less that must be worked into this first paragraph.
- **Introduce the love interest or villain (whichever is appropriate)**: Craft your second paragraph for this character in much the same way you did your first. You can also shave it down to one powerful standalone sentence to maximize impact and increase the pacing in the query. (See query sample below for example.)
- **Stay on track**: The paragraph revealing what goes wrong and how the conflict escalates needs to be a lean, trim thing of elegant power. Think of it as building a pyramid. Lay your foundational sentence (what thrusts the main characters into conflict), build with a sentence about how that conflict gets worse, and finish with the event that pushes your characters irrevocably into your book's final showdown. Weave together emotion and action the same way you do in your story. Don't neglect your character's emotional responses to the escalating

conflict, but don't stop building the conflict to let the characters reflect on their state of mind.

- **Wrap it up with a call to action sentence or question**: In the final paragraph of your hook (which you must also keep down to 2-3 sentences), state the nearly insurmountable problem in front of your hero and heroine, what they must do to overcome it, and what they lose if they fail. i.e. "Sarah must find a way to defeat the Kingdom of Hell and reverse the ancient curse running through her blood before she becomes the next Chosen."

- **Finish with your stats paragraph**: Unless you've decided to open with your stats paragraph, this is the moment when you deliver a nice, clean exit from your query. i.e. "CHOSEN is a young adult paranormal complete at 70,000 words. I'm impressed with your sales record in the young adult genre and with your agency's emphasis on building long-term careers. I look forward to hearing from you."

Now, you know what to include in your query and how to structure it. The only element missing is how to judge if you've done a good job of writing a hook that accurately represents your story and grabs a reader's interest. If you'd like some help in this area, I suggest running your completed hook by a few people who've never read your book and whom you can trust to be honest with you. Ask them to explain the characters and story to you after they've read your hook. You'll quickly see where you have significant gaps or misconceptions. Also, ask them if they feel a connection to the characters and if the conflict is one that makes them want to read more. If they're hesitant, you have work to do.

## Sample Query Letter

This is the query letter that landed me my agent. You'll notice that while I keep the escalation of conflict moving forward as I taught you, I play with the four paragraph structure. Using fragments and standalone statements increases the pacing and delivers my Voice.

Ms. Fabulous Agent
1234 Publishable Ave.
New York City, NY 10001

Dear Ms. Agent,

Living in New York City can be murder.

Alexa Tate is more than human. She can swim underwater without holding her breath, scale a brick building in five seconds flat, and sense the emotions of those about to commit a crime. A secretary by day, she uses her skills to hunt down evil at night. She is stronger, faster, and more lethal than anyone she's ever met.

Until now.

A non-human hunter has come to town. Using mind-control to inhabit his victims and through them commit unspeakable crimes, the hunter leaves a trail of bodies leading right to Alexa's door.

Suddenly, Alexa is the prey in an ancient war whose rules she is just beginning to understand.

To stop the hunter and save those she loves, she must uncover the truth about her origins, keep a certain handsome cop from suspecting her of crimes she may have committed, and unleash the tremendous power locked inside of her without becoming what she fears most: a killer.

Shadowing Fate is an urban fantasy complete at 80,000 words. I'm a member of RWA and a 2008 Golden Heart finalist. I look forward to hearing from you.

For more examples of query letters, go to http://queryshark.blogspot.com. You'll see examples of queries that are excellent, and queries that were revised until they became excellent.

## Workshopping a Query

To help you gain the tools necessary to take your query from first draft to polished perfection, I'm going to workshop a query letter here. Let's start by taking a look at the first draft:

### Draft One:

What would you do if everything you knew about the world wasn't true?

That's what happens when Sarah, a normal, ordinary seventeen-year-old high school senior who has always made good grades and had a lot of friends, finds out something that has been kept secret from her for her whole life. She comes home from school one day to find a stranger waiting for her who gives her a mark on the inner wrist just by touching her. Her best friend is Julia, another cheerleader, and Sarah just wants to graduate, go to a good college and hang out with Julia (and maybe the cute boy she sits next to in Physics), but now she can't. Her mark is getting darker.

The man who gave the mark to Sarah watches her. He knows the power running through her blood is something his leaders would do anything to have. Her time is running out. Soon the mark will be at full strength and she'll be the next Chosen.

CHOSEN is a paranormal young adult novel. I've been writing for most of my life, and while I don't have anything published yet, I did spend two years working on this and editing this, and I think you'll find it's as good as the other books on the bookstore shelf. If you think that it isn't, I'm willing to edit it however you think I should. I have a synopsis and sample chapters I can send if you request. I also have another novel I'm working on about a kingdom of trolls who need a human girl to be their queen. Thank you.

Comments:

- Starting with a generic, clichéd question isn't the best way to start strong. It's better to either make a strong statement that instantly grabs the reader's attention, or just dive right into the hook.

- We get the facts about Sarah's goals and life situation, along with the story set-up, but we don't get her emotional response to receiving the mark. I suggest streamlining the info about Sarah so we can spend a bit more time on the pivotal moment when her life changes.
- Does the man have a name? Was he just delivering a message, or does he have a larger agenda here? Does he mean her harm or good? Is he going to work with her to find a way out of this?
- What does it mean to be Chosen? It looks like this is a bad thing, but what will it cost Sarah? We need to truly understand the stakes.
- We also need to know what specifically Sarah (and the man, if he's working with her) have to do to stop this.
- I suggest moving the information about the stakes and what Sarah must do to avoid becoming the next Chosen into its own paragraph.
- The last paragraph needs to cover less ground. We don't need to know how long you spent writing this or that you don't have anything else published. We also don't need to know that you're willing to edit it. Instead, focus a sentence on why you are querying this agent. Finally, don't pitch another book in this query.

Draft Two:


Sarah Hightower—cheerleader, prom queen, and valedictorian of her senior class—has a secret that could kill her. Raised by her aunt and uncle in a small mountain town, Sarah dreams of bigger things. She wants to go to a prestigious university and become a world renowned physicist. She wants to see if the kiss she shared with Casey Miller on prom night might lead to a summer romance. And she desperately wants to pretend she can't hear voices whispering to her at night in a language she shouldn't be able to understand.

All her dreams, and her pretending, come crashing to a halt the day before graduation when a stranger shows up on her doorstep and marks her inner wrist simply by speaking one word. Terrified by the mark and by the fact that she can now hear the nighttime voices in the middle of the day, Sarah turns to her aunt and uncle for help.

It's the worst mistake she could ever make.

Declan MacLeod did his job. He marked the Potential, just as he's marked every other Potential each spring for the past one hundred years. It's a routine. A shot in the dark. None of the others he's been sent to mark ever understood his language. None of them heard the Kingdom. Until Sarah. He's as shocked as she is.

He should leave. Let the Kingdom come for her and look away as the precious gene floating through her blood buys his leaders another century of power. He should, but he can't. Instead, he helps her hide.

But no one hides from the Kingdom of Hell for long. Now, with less than a week before the gene in Sarah's blood reaches full strength, and with the entire might of Hell on their heels, Declan and Sarah must escape those who hunt them and assassinate the Kingdom's leaders before Sarah becomes the next Chosen.

CHOSEN is a young adult paranormal complete at eighty-five thousand words. I heard you speak at a recent SCBWI conference and am impressed with your sales record and your commitment to your clients. Thank you for your time.

Comments:
- Much better on giving us who Sarah is and how she feels!
- The query is just a bit too long, so you need to look for places where you can trim it down. The first paragraph might be an option. We need to know who Sarah is, but maybe just pick one or two important things to share so you can free up space.
- Why is turning to her aunt and uncle for help a mistake?
- Why does Declan decide to help her?
- You're almost there! It's coming together now.

Draft Three:


Sarah Hightower—cheerleader, prom queen, and valedictorian of her senior class—has a secret that could kill her. Raised by her aunt and uncle in a small mountain town, Sarah dreams of becoming a world renowned physicist. Maybe winning the Nobel Prize. But mostly, she dreams of a day when she can't hear voices whispering to her at night in a language she shouldn't be able to understand.

All her dreams die the day a strange boy shows up and marks her inner wrist simply by speaking one word. Terrified by the mark and by the fact that she can now hear the nighttime voices in the middle of the day, Sarah turns to her aunt and uncle for help.

It's the worst mistake she could ever make.

Declan MacLeod marked the Potential, just as he's marked every other Potential each spring for the past one hundred years. It's routine. A shot in the dark. None of the others he's been sent to mark ever understood his language. None of them could hear the Kingdom. Until Sarah. He's as shocked as she is.

He's supposed to leave. Let the Kingdom come for her and look away as the precious gene floating through her blood buys his leaders another century of power. But Declan isn't who the Kingdom thinks he is, and he has no intention of letting the rulers of Hell drain this girl dry. Instead, he helps her hide—from the Kingdom and from her family.

The very people who should be helping Declan protect Sarah have named her life forfeit, a debt owed for a pact made with the Kingdom of Hell long ago. When they report Declan's treachery, he too is marked as prey. Now, with less than a week before the gene in Sarah's blood reaches full strength, and with the entire might of Hell on their heels, Declan and Sarah must escape those who hunt them and defeat the Kingdom's leaders before Declan is executed and Sarah becomes the next Chosen.

CHOSEN is a young adult paranormal complete at eighty-five thousand words. I heard you speak at a recent SCBWI conference and am impressed with your sales record and your commitment to your clients. Thank you for your time.

## Comments:

- Good job getting all of the important story elements in the query!
- Even though the hook portion is longer than the suggested four paragraph structure, the pace and flow of the query will keep the reader engaged.

# Query-Building Worksheet

If you're having trouble narrowing down what to include in your hook, use this worksheet to help you prioritize the information. This worksheet works best if you keep your answers as concise as possible.

1. Concept Sentence: _____ must _____ to _____ but _____ is a huge problem.
2. Main Character #1:_____
   a. Two-three personality traits that define this character:_____
   b. Agenda (What one thing does your character truly want?):_____
   c. Reaction (How does your character feel when villain or obstacle thwarts agenda for the first time?):_____ _____
   d. Response (What action does your character take to address problem of villain or obstacle?):_____ _____
3. Main Character #2:_____

     a. Two-three personality traits that define this character:_____

     b. Agenda (What one thing does your character truly want?):_____

     c. Reaction (How does your character feel when villain or obstacle thwarts agenda for the first time?):_____

        _____

     d. Response (What action does your character take to address problem of villain or obstacle?):_____

        _____

4. Label the problem (The villain or the nearly insurmountable obstacle between the hero/heroine and what he/she wants):_____

     ____

     a. Significant secondary problem (If one exists):_____

     b. Significant secondary problem (If one exists):_____

5. The stakes (What are the consequences if the hero/heroine fails to defeat the villain or obstacle?):_____

     _____

6. What must the hero/heroine do to defeat the villain or overcome the obstacle? (Keep list to 3 items max):_____

     _____

# Worksheet Example

I've filled out the Query-Building Worksheet using the query for CHOSEN that I workshopped earlier so you can see how each fact in the query has a place in the worksheet. If it doesn't fit on the worksheet, it doesn't go in the query.

1. Concept Sentence: __Sarah & Declan___ must ___escape those who hunt them & assassinate the leaders of Hell___ to ___save their lives__ but _betrayal and the army of Hell__is a huge problem.
2. Main Character #1:__Sarah Hightower_____
   a. Two-three personality traits that define this character: _Ambitious, smart, scared__
   b. Agenda (What one thing does your character truly want?): _To be free of the mark so she can be a normal girl__
   c. Reaction (How does your character feel when villain or obstacle thwarts agenda for the first time?):___Terrifed_____
   _
   d. Response (What action does your character take to address problem of villain or obstacle?):___Asks her aunt and uncle for help_____
3. Main Character #2:___Declan MacLeod_____

a. Two-three personality traits that define this character: _**Secretive, Loyal, Determined**_

b. Agenda (What one thing does your character truly want?): _**To destroy the Kingdom of Hell**_

c. Reaction (How does your character feel when villain or obstacle thwarts agenda for the first time?):__**Determined and afraid**_____

d. Response (What action does your character take to address problem of villain or obstacle?):_ **Goes on the run w/Sarah and plans to assassinate Hell's leaders**_____

4. <u>Label the problem (The villain or the nearly insurmountable obstacle between the hero/heroine and what he/she wants)</u>:__**The leaders of the Kingdom of Hell want Sarah's blood and know Declan is a traitor**_____

    a. Significant secondary problem (If one exists):__**Betrayal by Sarah's aunt and uncle**_____

    b. Significant secondary problem (If one exists):__**Mark is getting darker because Sarah's blood is almost ready & it makes her easier to track**_____

5. <u>The stakes (What are the consequences if the hero/heroine fails to defeat the villain or obstacle?)</u>:__**Death for them both and the leaders**

**of Hell get another century of unbridled power**_____

6. <u>What must the hero/heroine do to defeat the villain or overcome the obstacle? (Keep list to 3 items max)</u>:__**Evade the army of Hell and assassinate the leaders**_____

## Your Query Checklist

Before you hit "send," you need to double-check all of the following:

- **<u>Always address the agent or editor correctly</u>**: Spelling the agent's name wrong or using a generic "To Whom It May Concern" screams "I didn't do my research" and makes you look like an amateur. Research the agents you want to approach, make sure they are currently accepting submissions in your genre and that they've sold books in the last year, and then address them correctly.

- **<u>Send individual queries</u>**: No mass cc or forwards when you e-query. Agents understand you'll be querying others simultaneously, but getting a query with fifty other agents in the To: line makes it seem like the writer didn't do the research to understand which agents would be a good fit.

- **<u>Only send what the agent wants to see</u>**: All agents have different submission guidelines. It takes thirty seconds to read the submission guidelines on each agent's website and tailor your submission package to match. I had a query, a synopsis, and the first three chapters of my manuscript ready to go so whatever the agent wanted, I could easily send it. DO NOT make the mistake of seeing that an agent wants five sample pages and sending them fifty pages instead. An agent can tell if he or she likes your writing by reading a few pages, and now you've just shown them you can't follow simple directions very well. Or that you think you're above the rules. Neither of those will make you a good candidate to work with.

- **Proofread your query**: Then proofread it again. Read it aloud. You'll be amazed at the errors you'll catch. This is your first impression. Don't blow it by sending a query riddled with mechanical errors, misspelled words, or convoluted sentences. Your query needs to be as polished as your manuscript. Take the time to make it so.

- **Use correct business letter format if querying by hard copy:** If you don't know how to do this, Google a template or use one included in your Word program. It's essential that you give your complete contact information, and that you make the entire page look professional. Make sure to include a SASE for the agent's response. If you're e-querying, it's acceptable to use appropriate e-mail formatting, but be sure to include your contact information at the end with your signature.

- **Be careful how you stand out:** If you can imagine it, some writer has done it: sending queries on scented, colored paper, in envelopes marked

"Urgent" or filled with confetti, or queries that arrived with gifts for the agent. I've also seen instances where a writer claimed one of the agent's clients had referred the writer even though the client never actually offered that. Don't do any of this. You want to stand out by being more talented and more professional than the rest. You will gain attention by having a unique voice and a well-written book. Leave the confetti for your birthday party. Besides, if your writing isn't yet up to par, all the confetti in the world won't buy you a contract.

- **<u>Remain professional at all times</u>:** You will get rejection letters. Some will be nicer than others. Rejections come for a variety of reasons. Maybe the agent just signed a similar project. Maybe you just didn't "wow" the agent enough, but you will the next agent you query. Maybe you need to get a hard-nosed critique partner and rewrite your manuscript. Maybe your idea has been done too often, and your take isn't unique enough. Whatever the reason, be professional in your response. Don't email to ask an agent to be more specific in their response. Don't slay them verbally on Twitter, Facebook, or your blog. Just move on.

- **<u>Avoid the following mistakes</u>:**
  - Don't pitch more than one project at a time. If you want to mention that your book is the first in a series or that you're working on something else, find a way to do it that doesn't qualify as a double pitch. Usually, this can be worked into the stats paragraph.

i.e. "While DEFIANCE can stand alone as a novel, it is the first in a planned series."

- Don't compare yourself to other authors. Saying "I am the next J.K. Rowling" gives the impression that you have a huge ego and might be difficult to work with. It also screams "Amateur!" And if your writing sample doesn't hold up your claim, you end up looking incredibly foolish. It's fine to compare the voice and tone of your work to other comparable authors as a way for agents to understand where your book might fit in the market, however. i.e. "Readers of Kristin Cashore and Robin McKinley will enjoy reading DEFIANCE."
- Don't say you're better than what is on the market today. We've all picked up a book and thought, "Sheesh. I can write better than this." Maybe you can, but professional correspondence isn't the place to bring it up. Besides, someone might one day read your work and think the same thing. Let your writing speak for itself.
- Don't tell the agent you have a life-changing book, or an important book, or anything that smacks of hyperbole. If it's life-changing or important, the agent or editor is certainly smart enough to decide that for themselves. At best, you've set their expectations very high. At worst, saying things like this makes you look like you don't visit reality very

often, and that makes you a risky business partner.

- o  Never tell the agent how long you've been writing, that writing is your passion, that your very soul cries out for the written word, that your students/children loved the book, or that this is the book of your heart. All of that may be true, but guess what? It's true for every other writer in the slush pile, and not only does it fail to help you stand out, it wastes space you need for your hook. Plus, it doesn't sound professional. Save the gushing about your passion for when an agent calls to offer representation.
- o  Don't tell an agent that others keep rejecting this project. In fact, unless you've been previously represented by an agent who has submitted this project to editors (In which case, an agent would need to see that submissions list before knowing if he or she can offer representation.), don't mention its track record at all.
- o  Don't dare an agent to take you on or threaten that if you don't hear from them soon, you'll shop it around elsewhere. Agents expect you to be doing simultaneous submissions anyway.  Threatening, asking if they have the guts to rep you, or daring them to be brave enough to take on your project makes you sound like a rank amateur who will be difficult to work with.

- Avoid asking rhetorical questions. ("What would you do if the world as you knew it no longer existed?") or using tired clichés. ("the challenge of a lifetime," "like she never expected" etc.) The more specific to your project you can be, the better chance you have of convincing an agent you've got something fresh and marketable on your hands.

## What To Do While You Query

You've done your research, polished your query, and sent it out to a selection of agents. Now what? Here are a few things to keep in mind:

- **Wait times**: Publishing moves slowly in most cases. Even after you sign with an agent, or sign a book deal, publishing is a whole lot of hurry up and wait. The querying process is good practice for this. Wait times vary by agent, but most agents take 8-10 weeks to work through their query slush pile. Many agents will post their approximate response time, but you shouldn't take that as a definite. Remember, a good agent always puts his or her signed clients ahead of everything else. This may sometimes be frustrating to a querying writer, but it's the sign of a solid agent.
- **No response means no**: Many agents who have large client lists are unable to take the time to

personally reject every query they decide to pass on. Every agent I've known who has eventually adopted this policy did so with regret. Agents generally love writers and respect the process. But again, an agent must devote the lion's share of his or her work day to signed clients. That leaves very little time for individual query responses. If you're uncomfortable with this policy, do your research to identify agents who always respond.

- **When to nudge**: I'm often asked when it's appropriate to nudge an agent who has your query. The answer is never. If you feel strongly the agent didn't receive it (You never received the agent's auto-response confirming receipt, or the agent has a policy of always responding and recently posted that he or she is caught up on all query responses), you may send it again. But most of the time, if you've queried and not heard back in ten weeks, it's time to query another agent with this particular project. You can, however, nudge an agent on partial and full requests. Each agent works a on a slightly different timeline for reading partials and fulls, but I believe three months is a fair amount of time to give before nudging the agent with a polite inquiry as to the status of your manuscript. If you're reading this and thinking that by the time you wait ten weeks for a response on your query and another three months on a read of your partial, half a year will be gone, you're right. That's why you continue to query regularly until you find the right agent for you!

- **Send new queries:** While you're in the querying process, you should constantly be researching and adding agents to the list of those you'd like to query. Every time you receive a rejection, turn around and send out another query. It doesn't matter how many "no's" you get. It only matters that you don't quit before you get a "yes."
- **Write:** By far the most important (and most overlooked!) thing to do while querying is to write another book. For one, the work will keep your mind occupied so you obsess less about how your queries are being received. For another, if no one ends up requesting this particular book, pretty soon you'll have another one ready to query. I strongly advise you to write an entirely new project, not the next book in the series you're currently querying. If no one is interested in this book and all you've written is its sequel, you have nothing new to send out. If you have two polished manuscripts and you land an agent with your second, you have another series to discuss once you're represented.

## What To Ask An Agent

When you finally do receive an email from an agent asking to set up a phone call, you should probably have an oxygen tank handy. If you're anything like me, the inside of your stomach will act as though you've just hurtled yourself off a cliff, and the queasy, giddy joy inside of you will momentarily make you forget important bodily functions. Like breathing. And how to speak in a coherent fashion.

Hopefully, you'll regain at least some of your equilibrium before the phone call. But even if you don't, you're going to be super prepared so a little thing like nerves or overwhelming emotion won't derail you. It's important to have a few things handy for this conversation.

- **Privacy**: I have a busy household. Privacy is a rare gift, but I made sure I had it. I didn't want to be constantly interrupted by kids when I needed to focus. If you can't make that happen at home, take the call at a local coffee shop.
- **Notepad and pen**: You'll want to take notes. You'll want to remember the wonderful things the agent says about your book, jot down any stray thoughts or questions you want to bring up before the end of the conversation, and write down any issues/ideas/thoughts the agent brings to the table about your book and your career.
- **Career plan**: You need to be able to discuss where you would like to be in the next five years (or more.) The agent needs to understand your goals and how you plan to get there. And you need to hear from the agent how he or she can help you achieve those goals.
- **Questions**: You need a list of questions that you'd like to ask. Type them up and leave enough space beneath them to take notes on the agent's answer. I'm going to give you a solid list of possible questions, but there may be others you'd like to add.

- **Answers**: The agent will have questions for you as well. Some of those will center on your book and possibly your openness to the editorial direction the agent thinks would get it in the best shape for submission. Some will be about your communication preferences, your online presence, your writing style … anything that the agent needs to know to see if the two of you would be a good fit. Be prepared, and be absolutely honest. It doesn't help to pretend to be what you think the agent is looking for. You need a solid working relationship and that can't work if you've set unrealistic expectations about yourself.

## List of Questions

Here is a list of questions you may want to ask an agent while discussing possible representation. Not all of these will apply to you, some you should already know the answers to based on your research, and you may think of others you'd like to add.

- How long have you been an agent?
- What is your pre-agenting background?
- What is your commission rate on domestic sales? Foreign sales? Who pays for phone calls, copy fees, and mail or messenger fees to send the manuscript to editors?
- Does your agency have a contract? (Read this very carefully before signing.)

- If we decide in the future to part ways, how do you expect that to be handled?
- How long does it generally take you to read your client's work? Return phone calls/emails?
- Do you respond to your clients seven days a week or Mon-Fri?
- How long does it take you to send out royalty statements? Do you send originals or copies?
- Do you help me edit the manuscript before going on submission?
- Will we discuss ahead of time the editors you'd like to submit this project to?
- How often will you keep me up to date on how the submissions process is going? Will you pass rejection letters on to me directly or summarize them for me?
- Do you make multiple submissions? What submissions plan do you see working for my book?
- Do you have agency staff dedicated to handling contracts, foreign rights, and/or film rights? If not, how are those handled?
- Do you have an assistant or do you handle all of your own calls and correspondence?
- How can you help me build a long-term career? What opportunities do you think we should watch for to help me reach my goals?
- How many books a year do you think I can sell? (If you're writing series or category.)
- How many clients do you represent? How many of those are in my genre?

- May I speak with a few of your clients? (This allows you to discuss the agent's communication style, response time, and what those clients love about this agent to get a feel for whether this is a good fit for you.)
- What recent sales have you made? What houses have you sold to?
- Would you like to see my other completed manuscripts?
- Do you want a completed manuscript from me for future submissions, or would you rather have a proposal?
- If I have multiple projects, who decides which projects are submitted to publishers?
- How many books do you expect me to write each year? What if I want to write more or less?
- If I'd like to publish in multiple genres, would you be willing to handle that?
- Do you have houses or editors you prefer to use? Any you refuse to use?
- Do you take an editorial approach to your clients' manuscripts, or do you prefer to simply submit and then negotiate for the best contract possible?
- How many rounds of submissions will you do before deciding to pull a project from submission?
- Are you open to my suggestions regarding which houses or editors I'd prefer to work with?
- What contingency do you have in place to deal with outstanding contracts, process royalties, or deal with other business related to my career in the event of death, injury, or long-term illness?

- Will other agents at the agency have input on my manuscript or submissions list?
- What do you expect from me as a client?
- Why do you think I'd be a good client for you?
- Why do you feel you'd be the right agent for me?

## How To Handle Multiple Offers

You've spent all of this effort researching and querying with the sole intent of snagging a literary agent's attention. So what do you do with that attention if other agents still have your query or a partial/full?

You leverage it into the opportunity for multiple offers of representation.

If an agent expresses interest in representing you, he or she will most likely ask if you have other agents you need to talk with before accepting. If you have material out with others, you need to take the time to approach them. A simple email letting them know that you now have an offer on the table will give those agents a chance to move quickly on your query or partial/full. It's acceptable to give every agent involved a time limit. I suggest letting the offering agent know you'll give them your answer within a week. Then set a smaller time frame with those who still have your material. If another agent is interested, you will have time to discuss it and think through your decision.

Please note that getting a request for a partial or full does not mean you need to nudge other agents to move on your query.

The only time you let agents know of competing interest is when you have an offer on the table.

What happens if you have more than one agent interested in representing you? This is where your careful preparation comes in handy. Ask your questions. Thoroughly go over your career plan and the agent's submission plan for your project. Compare communication styles. Sales records. Enthusiasm and experience. Agency practices. Response times. How many clients an agent already has. And don't forget to include that gut level response you felt as you talked personally with the agent. Did you find the agent intimidating or welcoming? Did you find yourself unable to explain your points in a way the agent seemed to intuitively understand or were you constantly on the same page?

You might really like more than one agent. Certainly you have a high level of respect for each agent or you wouldn't have queried them. But in the end, it comes down to you. Your career. What you want from the agent/client relationship. You're going into business for the long-haul with someone. Make sure you choose the partner that fits you best. And though it's hard, let go of the guilt you might feel at turning down one of the agents. It's a business, and you made a business decision. The agent understands that, and a good agent will never hold that against you.

## Hold Out For The Right Agent

I'll keep this short and simple. Having NO agent is far better than having the WRONG agent. For one, working with the wrong agent wastes time you could've spent working with someone who would be an excellent partner. For another, having the wrong agent submit your work all over the place cuts down significantly on what another agent can do for you. Finally, working with the wrong agent and going through the decision to end the relationship is emotionally difficult.

How do you avoid signing with the wrong agent? Here are some guidelines:

- **Don't be desperate**. I know how it feels to query for years and get nowhere. You get to a point where you think any literary agent who isn't in jail and seems halfway interested in your work is better than nothing. Don't fall for this way of thinking. How do you beat feeling desperate? Keep taking positive action. Write the next book. Query the next agent. Chin up and keep your standards high.
- **Watch for red flags**. Remember that list of red flags I gave you earlier? Study it. Learn it. And back away when you find those. If something is wrong before you sign, it's only going to get worse after.
- **Listen to your instincts**: An agent may be the world's loveliest person. The fiercest negotiator. A warrior on the sales front. And might still be absolutely wrong for you. If you don't feel completely confident in your chemistry with a prospective agent, if you worry the agent doesn't "get" your career goals, or isn't communicating with you the way you prefer to work, it's okay to

say "no." The good news is an industry professional has now recognized that you are publishable. The better news is you listened to your instincts and avoided the complications of disengaging from the wrong agent/client relationship for you. If this agent recognized your talent, another will recognize it too.

## No One Wants This Book. Now What?

Sometimes, you query and query and query, and you receive nothing but rejections. Maybe some of the rejections gave you limited feedback on the reasons why. Maybe some were form rejections. You're discouraged, and you feel like you're at the end of the road with this book.

Now what?

First, let's take an honest look at some of the main reasons agents or editors reject a manuscript:

- Quality of the writing: There's a lot of competition in publishing. Your writing has to be polished and compelling. If you're querying one of your first few books, there's a good chance your writing isn't at the level it needs to be to compete. That doesn't have to be discouraging. We all suck when we start! There's a learning curve. A smart writer keeps working on craft until the writing becomes exceptional.

- <u>Lack of conflict or conflict doesn't push far enough</u>: Do you have a strong antagonist or villain? Are the obstacles in your hero's path nearly insurmountable? Will it cost him something to succeed? Or have you been easy on him? Too afraid to push? Look at the best sellers list. Regardless of genre, those books all have one thing in common: strong conflict, either internal, external, or both.
- <u>Poor genre sales</u>: Some genres are flourishing while others are struggling. If you write in a genre where only established authors are selling enough to be worth a publisher's investment, your idea and your writing will have to be truly above the bar to gain interest. An agent doesn't mind a challenge, but he or she has to feel confident it's a challenge that can be overcome.
- <u>High or low word count</u>: Remember when I told you to Google accepted industry standard word counts for your genre? I was serious. If you're clinging to your 155k novel because, darn it, Stephen King publishes in that length, you need a reality check. Pay your dues. Prove your worth as a storyteller and business investment. THEN you can discuss lengthy word counts with your editor.
- <u>Idea is overdone</u>: Maybe your idea just doesn't stand out from the crowd of other books in your genre. If so, it's back to the drawing board for you, and it's time to let your creativity run free. I suggest reading outside your genre for the kind of out of the box inspiration you can then bring back to your genre.

- Didn't connect: Your writing can be excellent, and your idea can be solid, but if an agent doesn't fall in love with the book enough to be excited to fight for a great contract, he or she will pass.
- Too similar: Your book may be too similar to a book the agent already represents. If so, he or she might pass on it because the list of viable editors to submit to have already been exhausted, or because he or she worries about a conflict of interest.

If your book isn't succeeding on the query circuit, there are some options you can pursue:

- **Determine if the problem is your query or your book**: Submit your query to www.queryshark.com or www.evileditor.blogspot.com and get professional feedback. Or ask people in your writer's group to read your query and tell you what your book is about and if they'd buy it based solely on that description. If the problem is your query, revise. If the problem is the book, either send it through a critique partner or two (find one at your local writer's group, on writing loops, or in online writing communities) and do some serious revising, or move on to the next.
- **Work on the next book**: Remember how I advised you to be writing the next book while you queried? Now that work is about to pay off. You can focus all the lessons you just learned about craft and querying on this new project. Revise and polish this

book until you feel it far exceeds the last book you queried. Then write another query and begin the process again. And don't forget to write another new book while you query!

- **Try smaller presses**: There are a variety of small presses who accept unagented submissions. If you suspect the problem is market-based, you may decide submitting your book to some of these is the right decision for you.

- **Self-publishing**: There are a growing number of writers going the self-publishing route. There are some exciting opportunities available, but the decision to do so has to line up with your career goals. Self-publishing isn't a short cut. If the reason you received rejections from agents and editors is the quality of your writing, you will struggle to find an audience with readers as well. However, if you feel confident your writing is up to par and the entrepreneurial aspects of self-publishing appeal to your inner executive, approach it with careful research and planning as you would any business venture.

Querying is not for the faint of heart, but neither is a career in publishing. No matter your results, no matter your career choices, I wish you all the best on your journey and encourage you, above all else, to keep writing.

47176358R00033

Made in the USA
Lexington, KY
05 August 2019